Tynnwyd o'r stoc
Withdrawn

RISING ★ STARS

Rising Stars UK Ltd.
22 Grafton Street, London W1S 4EX
www.risingstars-uk.com

NASEN House, 4/5 Amber Business Village, Amber Close, Amington,
Tamworth, Staffordshire B77 4RP

Every effort has been made to trace copyright holders and obtain their permission for the use of copyright materials. The publisher will gladly receive information enabling them to rectify any error or omission in subsequent editions.

All facts are correct at time of going to press.

The right of Andy Seed to be identified as the author of this work has been asserted by him in accordance with the Copyright, Design and Patents Act 1988.

Published 2008

Text, design and layout © Rising Stars UK Ltd.
Series Consultant: Lorraine Petersen
Cover design: Neil Straker Creative
Cover photograph: Alamy
Design: Geoff Rayner, Bag of Badgers
Editorial: Frances Ridley
Illustrations: Bill Greenhead for Illustration Ltd.
Photographs:
AKG: 8, 11, 12, 13, 14, 19, 26-27, 30, 32-33, 34, 35, 38, 40, 41, 42, 46, 47
Alamy: 4, 36
Kobal Collection: 20, 22, 24, 28-29, 39, 45
VinMag Archive: 10, 44

British Library Cataloguing in Publication Data.
A CIP record for this book is available from the British Library.

ISBN: 978-1-84680-442-7

Printed by: Craftprint International Ltd, Singapore

CONTENTS

ANIMATION: THE BIG PICTURE

Lots of people enjoy funny or cool cartoons on TV. These are animations. In animations, pictures or models seem to move.

FOCUS

FIND OUT THE ANSWERS TO THESE QUESTIONS.

1   WHAT YEAR DID STEAMBOAT WILLIE COME OUT?

2   WHAT IS STOP-MOTION?

3   WHAT DOES HOMER SIMPSON HATE?

ZOOMING IN...

2001
Shrek
Anything can happen with computer cartoons.

1989
Wallace and Gromit
Nutty fun with the daft duo.

1989
The Simpsons
D'oh! Homer takes over the world.

1928
Steamboat Willie
A mouse becomes a star.

1940s
Tom and Jerry
Cat and mouse comedy.

1963
Jason and the Argonauts
See skeletons come to life!

1980s
Anime cartoons
From drawing to film.

CARTOONS COME TO LIFE

THE FIRST ANIMATIONS WERE SHOWN AT THE CINEMA. THEY WERE IN BLACK AND WHITE AND THEY HAD NO SOUND.

IN 1928, A FILM CALLED STEAMBOAT WILLIE CAME OUT. ITS STAR WAS MICKEY MOUSE AND HE COULD TALK!

See the new star of the screen

MICKEY MOUSE!

in the cartoon with sound

STEAMBOAT WILLIE

A film by Walt Disney

Watch him have fun on the river!

Meet his girlfriend Minnie!

Hear him play music on a cow!

See him run from Captain Pete!

Don't miss Mickey He's the funniest mouse in town!

WALT DISNEY AND MICKEY MOUSE

Steamboat Willie was a big hit for Walt Disney. It was the first animation with sound.

Mickey Mouse became a star! He appeared in more than 120 cartoons and he had his own TV show.

HOW DISNEY MADE ANIMATIONS

1   Artists made thousands of pictures.

2   A camera filmed the pictures one at a time.

3   The film was run at speed.

4   The pictures blended together and seemed to move.

FUN FACT

WALT DISNEY WAS SCARED OF MICE!

SHORT AND WACKY

TOM AND JERRY CARTOONS WERE POPULAR IN THE 1940S AND 1950S.

IN EACH CARTOON, TOM THE CAT CHASES JERRY THE MOUSE.

THERE IS LOTS OF **CARTOON VIOLENCE** BUT NO BLOOD.

STORYBOARD

Artists draw storyboards to plan cartoons like this one.

Idea for a Tom and Jerry film: The Farm Cat

1. Tom is in a barn.

2. Jerry creeps past with a sack of corn.

3. Tom throws a pitchfork at Jerry.

4. Jerry twangs the **pitchfork** handle at Tom's head.

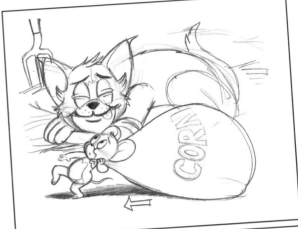

5. Tom chases Jerry into a chicken shed.

6. The hens kick eggs all over Tom.

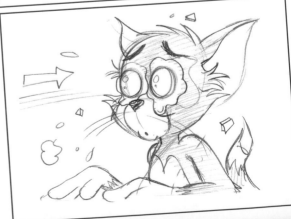

7. Jerry hides among some sheep.

8. Tom looks for him and bumps into a big ram with horns.

9. The ram chases Tom.

10. Jerry pulls two big carrots out of a field.

11. Tom grabs Jerry – Jerry whacks him with a carrot.

12. Tom's head gets stuck in a carrot hole.

13. Jerry gets the ram to charge at Tom.

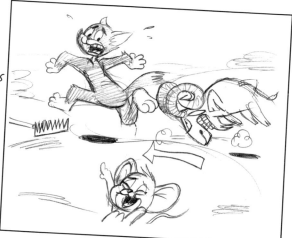

14. Tom goes flying.

15. Jerry has a big feast.

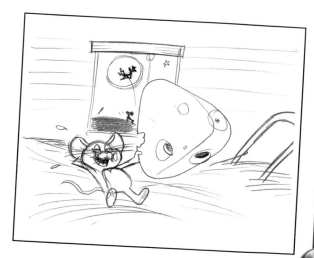

SIXTY YEARS OF CAT AND MOUSE

In the 1940s not many people had a TV.
They went to the cinema to watch cartoons.
Tom and Jerry were very popular.

QUIET PLEASE!

This film is a classic Tom and Jerry cartoon.

Title	*Quiet Please!*
Date	1945
Length	8 minutes
Type	Hand-drawn animation
Story	Spike the dog is trying to sleep. Tom keeps him awake by chasing Jerry. Spike gets blown up and blames Tom.
Trivia	Won an **Oscar** for Best Short Cartoon.

FILM FACT

TOM AND JERRY FILMS ARE
STILL POPULAR TODAY.

THEY ARE SHOWN ON TV
AND SOLD ON DVD.

FIGHTING SKELETONS!

MODELS CAN BE **ANIMATED** ON FILM, TOO.

THIS TYPE OF ANIMATION IS CALLED STOP-MOTION.

STOP-MOTION WAS USED IN JASON AND THE **ARGONAUTS** IN 1963.

IN THIS FILM, SKELETONS COME TO LIFE AND START FIGHTING!

Just seen a cool old film on DVD called Jason and the Argonauts!

Options   Back

What's it about?

Options   Back

1 ✉️oo   2 ABC   3 DEF

—€IIII
It's like a Greek **myth** with heroes, monsters and gods. Jason sails off in his ship to find the Golden **Fleece**.

Options

Sounds fun. What monsters are there?

Options   Back

—€IIII
There's a giant metal statue that comes to life. There's a beast called Hydra with 7 heads. The skeletons with swords are the best – well scary!

Options

Is it a cartoon?

Options   Back

—€IIII
No, it's got real actors. My dad says it was made before computer special effects.

Options

I wonder how they made the skeletons fight?

Options   Back

STOP-MOTION MAGIC

The skeletons in *Jason and the Argonauts* are small, bendy models. **SFX** expert Ray Harryhausen made them. He used stop-motion to bring them to life.

HOW HARRYHAUSEN MADE ANIMATIONS

1 The models were put into position.

2 The camera took a picture.

3 The models were moved a bit.

4 The camera took another picture.

5. This was repeated many times.

6. The film was run at speed. The pictures blended together and the models seemed to move.

FILM FACT

THE SKELETON FIGHT SCENE TOOK
FOUR AND A HALF MONTHS TO MAKE!

CLOSE UP:
THE WORLD OF ANIME

Anime are animations from Japan. They are made using computers.

FIRST, THE ARTIST DRAWS THE ANIME CHARACTER.

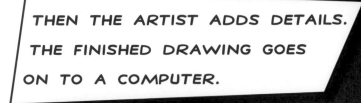

THEN THE ARTIST ADDS DETAILS. THE FINISHED DRAWING GOES ON TO A COMPUTER.

Anime characters have many **hallmark** features.

BIG HAIR

FANTASY CLOTHES

SLIM WAIST

LARGE EYES

SHARP CHIN

LONG LEGS

TV'S GREATEST FAMILY

IN 1989, A NEW CARTOON CAME ON TV. IT WAS CALLED THE SIMPSONS. IT TOOK THE WORLD BY STORM AND IS STILL GOING STRONG TODAY! PEOPLE LOVE THE CHARACTERS IN THE SHOW.

Homer Simpson

Age:
About 36

Appearance:
Bald, fat, unfit

Character:
Loud, rude, lazy, selfish, silly, clumsy

Job:
Nuclear power plant safety inspector

Likes:
Doughnuts, beer, his couch, TV, sleeping

Dislikes:
Work, salad, Mr Burns (his boss), exercise

Catchphrase:
"D'oh!"

Habits:
Watching TV all day; getting angry with son Bart

Greatest moment:
Going into space

Lisa Simpson

Age:

8

Appearance:

Small with spiky yellow hair

Character:

Clever, sensible, kind,
honest, musical,
sometimes annoying

Job:

Schoolgirl

Likes:

School,
Nelson Muntz (sometimes),
playing saxophone,
caring for animals

Dislikes:

Eating meat, low marks, people who are smarter
than her

Catchphrase:

"If anyone needs me I'll be in my room."

Habits:

Protesting, wearing pearls

Greatest moment:

Winning a trip to Washington

THE SIMPSONS

The Simpsons is popular because it's funny. It makes fun of people, places and ideas.

Over 400 episodes have been made and the show has won over 50 awards. *The Simpsons Movie* came out in 2007.

Cast list:

The Simpsons	Homer, Marge, Lisa, Bart, Maggie
Ned Flanders	neighbour
Krusty	TV clown
Apu	shopkeeper
Chief Wiggum	police officer
Mr Burns	rich villain
Principal Skinner	head teacher
Moe	bar owner

FUN FACT

BART SIMPSON HAS A WOMAN'S VOICE.
HE IS PLAYED BY THE ACTRESS
NANCY CARTWRIGHT.

NO CHEESE, GROMIT!

1989 WAS A GREAT YEAR FOR NICK PARK. HE FINISHED HIS FIRST WALLACE AND GROMIT FILM – A GRAND DAY OUT.

WALLACE IS AN INVENTOR AND GROMIT IS HIS DOG. IN THIS FILM, THEY FLY TO THE MOON TO LOOK FOR CHEESE.

CLEVER CLAYMATION!

Nick Park uses claymation to make his films. Claymation is like stop-motion but the models are made of clay. The models have movable metal frames inside. Each two seconds of film takes a day to make! The first three Wallace and Gromit films were 30 minutes long.

Then in 2005, the first Wallace and Gromit movie came out.
It was called *The Curse of the Were-Rabbit*.

FUN FACT

WALLACE AND GROMIT HAVE WON THREE OSCARS!

THE CURSE OF THE WERE-RABBIT

This film has all the hallmark Wallace and Gromit features.

COMIC FACES

SUPERB BACKGROUNDS

SILLY CHARACTERS

LARGE FEATURES

VERY 'ENGLISH' LOOK

WACKY INVENTIONS

GROMIT HAS NO MOUTH

FUNNY NAMES

WORD JOKES

REALISTIC TOUCHES

ANTI-PESTO
S.W.A.T. TEAM

HOP 2 IT

COMPUTER CREATURES

SHREK IS A GRUMPY GREEN **OGRE**.

HE HAS BEEN IN THREE FILMS.

A FOURTH FILM IS PLANNED FOR 2010.

THE SHREK FILMS ARE MADE BY

THE COMPANY **DREAMWORKS**.

Dear Film Buff Magazine,

I am a big fan of Shrek.
I love animated films because anything
can happen on screen.
I want to work on animated films
when I am older.
What jobs do people do at DreamWorks?
Best wishes,

Becky

Dear Becky,

Shrek is a great film. It took more than 275 people to make it. Some people wrote the **screenplay**. Other people made the characters and the **soundtrack**. Actors spoke the words for the characters. *Shrek* had two directors. A director makes sure that everything comes together.

There are hundreds of different jobs in animation – so keep working hard at school and your dream might come true.

Good luck!

Film Buff Magazine

COMPUTER ANIMATION

The Shrek films are made using special computers.
These computers cost £8000 each.
Artists create the characters and backgrounds
on the computers. Then they use them to **animate**
the characters.

FUN FACT

THE MAIN ACTORS IN SHREK NEVER MET
WHILE THEY WERE MAKING THE FILM.

Today, many animations are made using a computer.

It's much faster than the old way of doing things.

Computer animation is also used for special effects.

The *Lord of the Rings* and *Transformers* films both used computer animation.

GLOSSARY

Argonauts Men who sailed with Jason on his ship, The Argo.

Animate Make something move.

Animated Made to move.

Cartoon violence When characters in cartoons hit each other and blow each other up but no one gets hurt.

DreamWorks US film company.

Fantasy A kind of story about magic and adventure.

Fleece The woolly skin of a sheep.

Hallmark A feature that is very typical.

Myth An old story – many myths have heroes and monsters in them.

Ogre An ugly giant or monster found in stories.

Oscars Famous film awards.

Pitchfork A farm tool with a long handle – you lift straw with it.

Screenplay The words and directions for a film.

SFX Stands for 'special effects'. SFX make things look real in films.

Soundtrack The music and words for a film.

INDEX